W9-AUU-104

CASEBOOK
OF CRAZINESS

A N T O N I O
P R O H I A S

▪▬▬• ▪▬• ▬▬▬ •••• •• ▪▬ •••

FALL RIVER PRESS

New York

FALL RIVER PRESS

New York

An Imprint of Sterling Publishing
387 Park Avenue South
New York, NY 10016

FALL RIVER PRESS and the distinctive Fall River Press logo are
registered trademarks of Barnes & Noble, Inc.

Copyright © 1978 and 1982 by
Antonio Prohias and E.C. Publications, Inc.
All rights reserved
MAD, "Spy vs Spy," and all related elements ® and © by
E.C. Publications, Inc.

This compilation ©2014 E.C. Publications, Inc., published by Fall River Press, by arrangement with MAD Books.

Cartoon Network logo ™ and © by Cartoon Network.

Contents of this compilation appeared originally in slightly different form in
The Fifth MAD Report on Spy vs Spy and *The Sixth MAD Casebook on Spy vs Spy*.

All rights reserved. No part of this publication may be reproduced, stored in a retrieval
system, or transmitted in any form or by any means (including electronic, mechanical,
photocopying, recording, or otherwise) without prior written permission from the publisher.

ISBN 978-1-4351-5172-7

For information about custom editions, special sales, and premium and corporate purchases,
please contact Sterling Special Sales at 800-805-5489 or specialsales@sterlingpublishing.com.

Manufactured in the United States of America

2 4 6 8 10 9 7 5 3 1

www.sterlingpublishing.com

Visit MAD online at www.madmag.com

Though Alfred E. Neuman wasn't the first to say, "A fool and his money are soon parted," here's your chance to
prove the old adage right—subscribe to MAD! Simply call 1-800-4-MADMAG and mention code 5MBN2.
Operators are standing by (the water cooler).

CONTENTS

GO...!

FORWARD BY AUTHOR

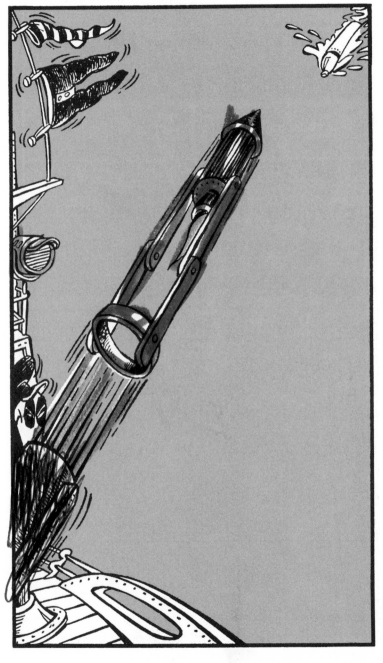

3

SPY VS SPY

4

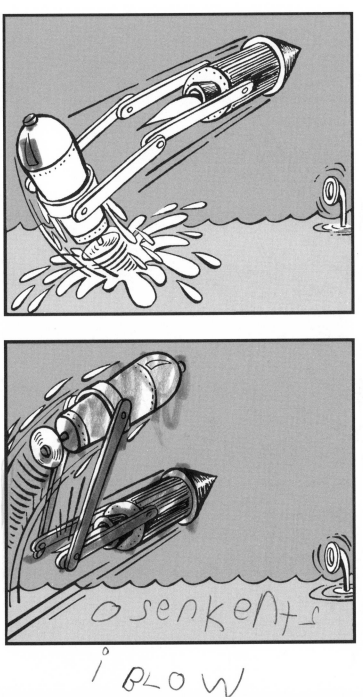

5

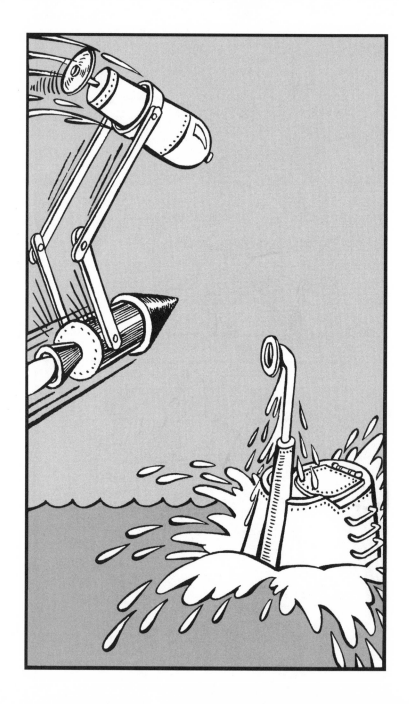

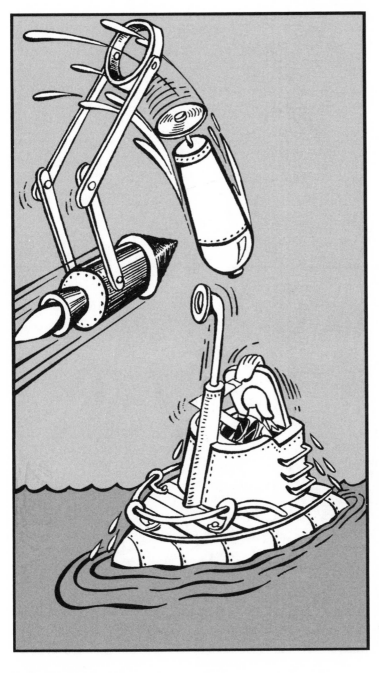

7

11

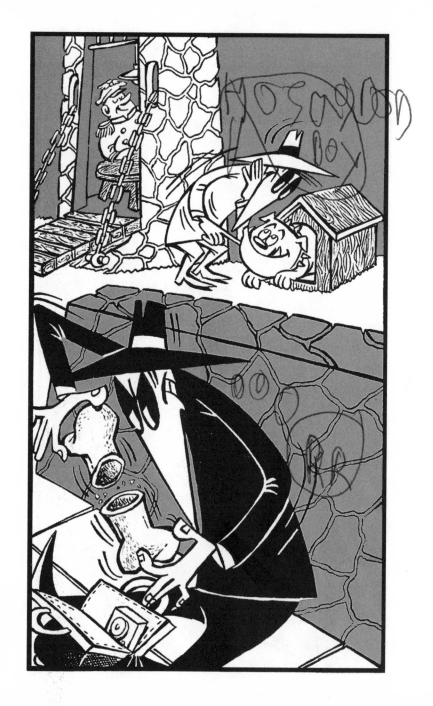

13

SPY VS SPY

14

15

17

TOP SECRET FILE 3

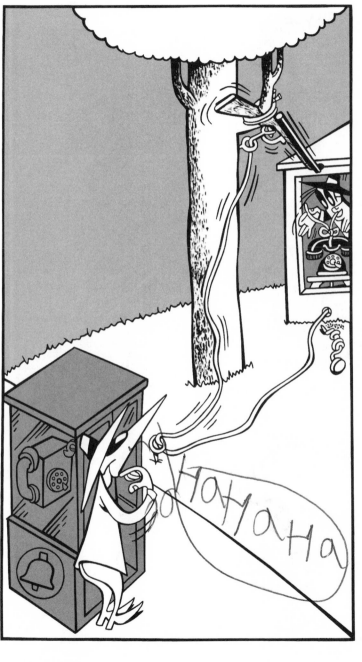

27

SPY VS SPY

28

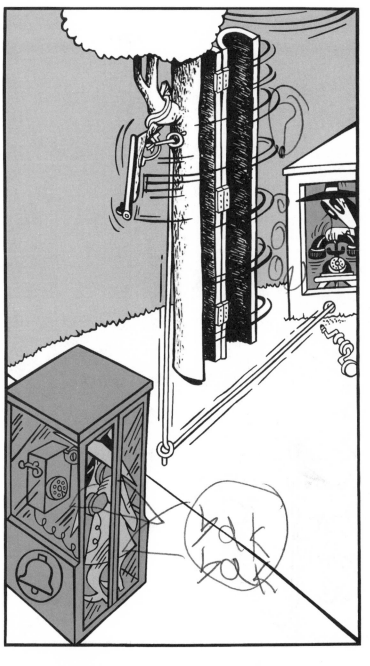

29

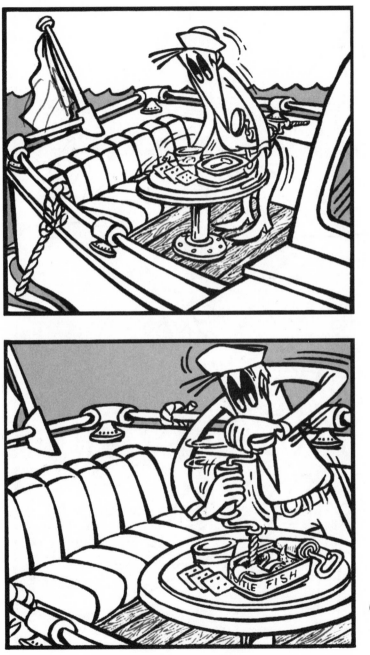

33

SPY VS SPY

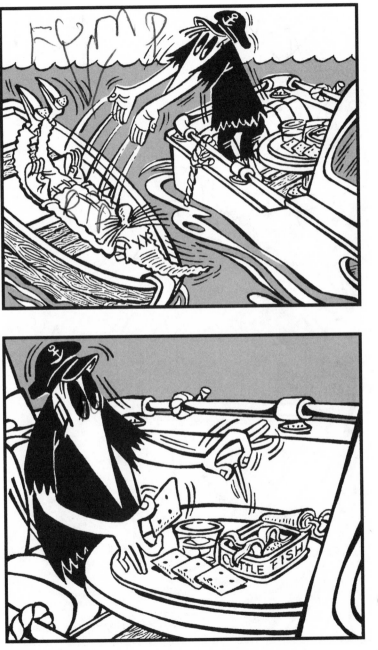

39

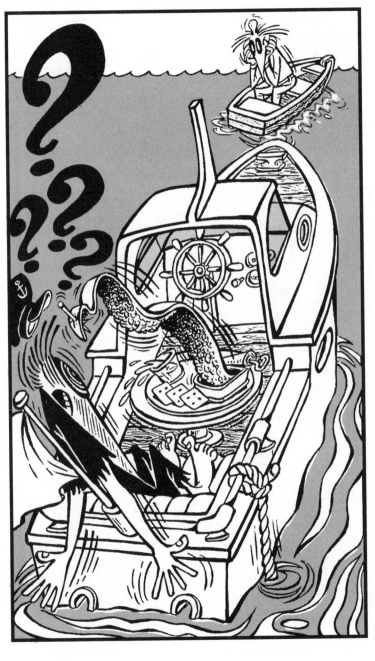

43

TOP SECRET FILE 5

49

52

TOP SECRET FILE 5

53

55

57

59

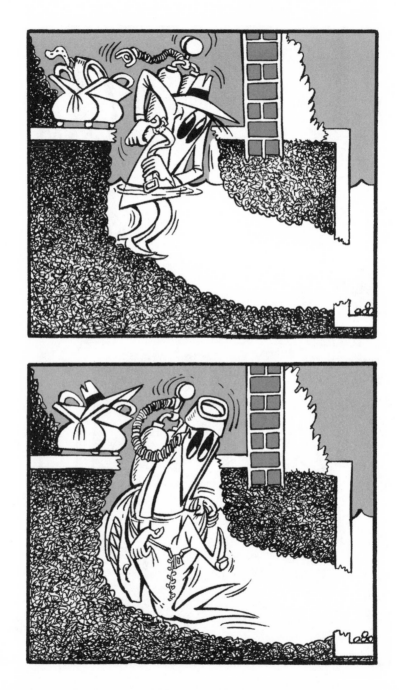

61

SPY VS SPY

68

SPY VS SPY

70

79

SPY VS SPY

82

83

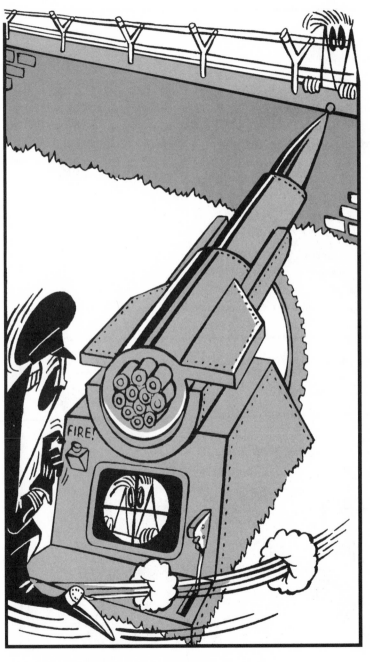

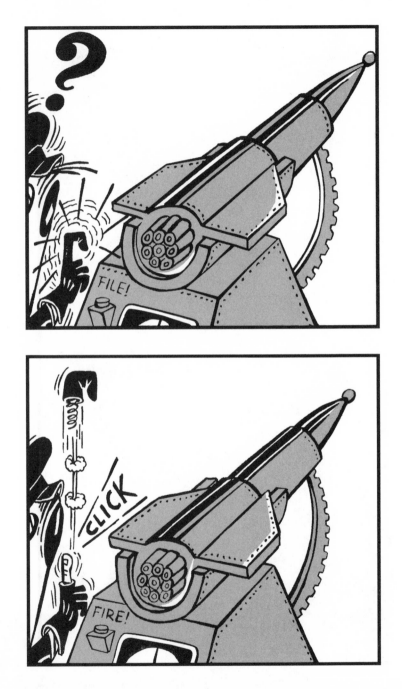

SPY VS SPY

86

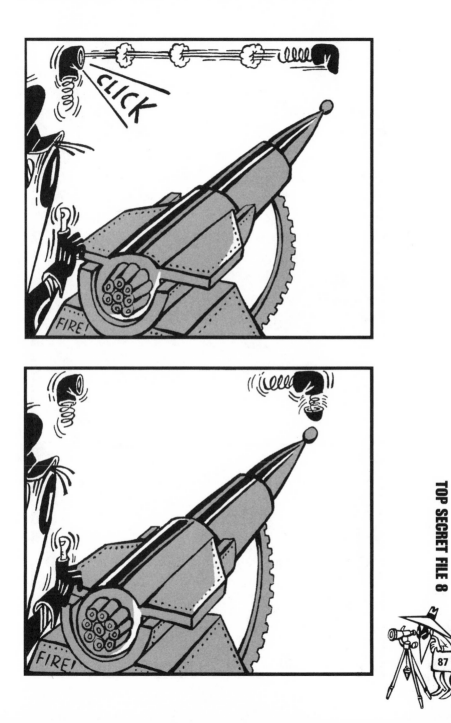

SPY VS SPY

88

89

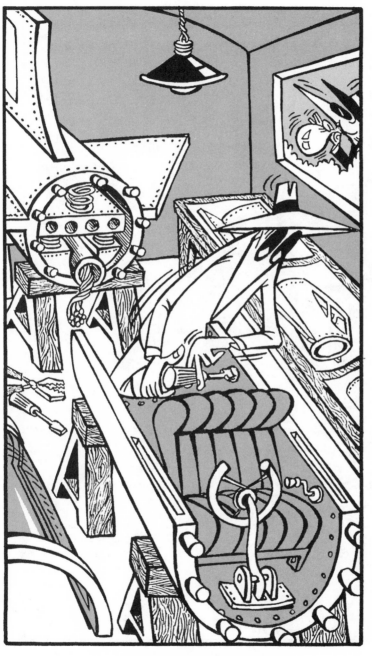

SPY VS SPY

94

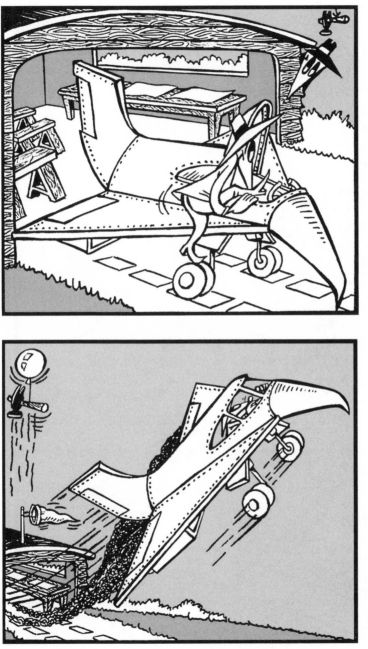

TOP SECRET FILE 9

95

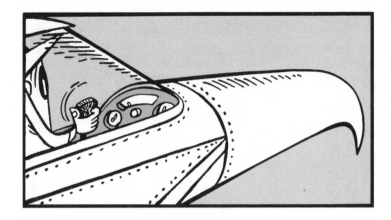

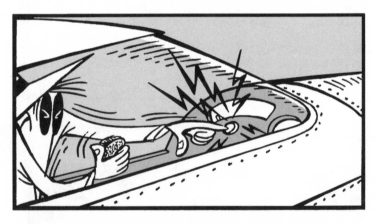

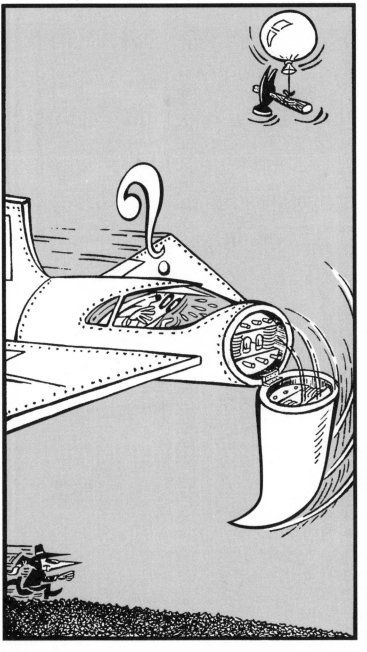

99

SPY VS SPY

100

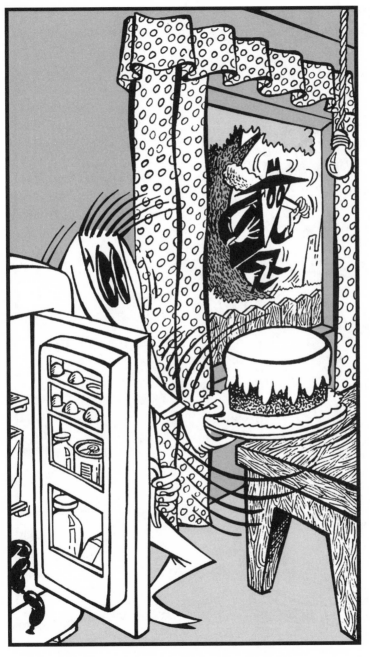

101

105

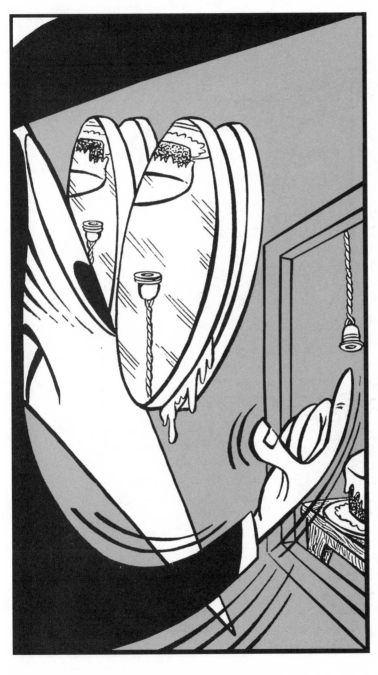

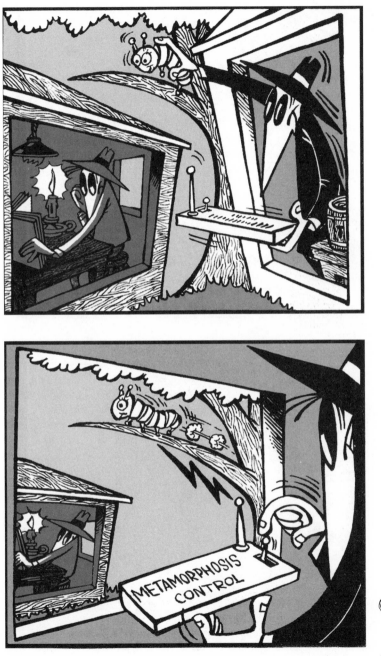

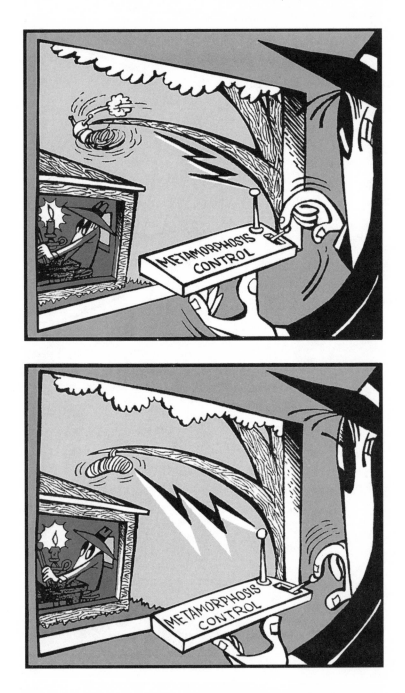

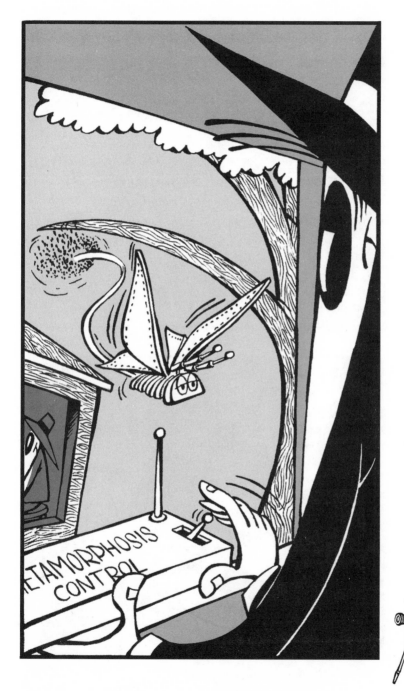

117

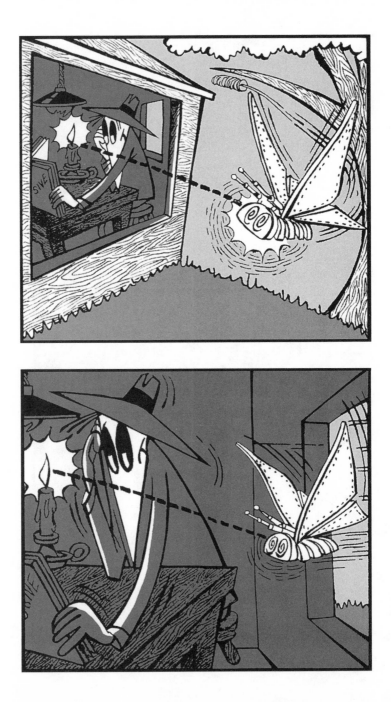

SPY VS SPY

118

123

129

131

SPY VS SPY

132

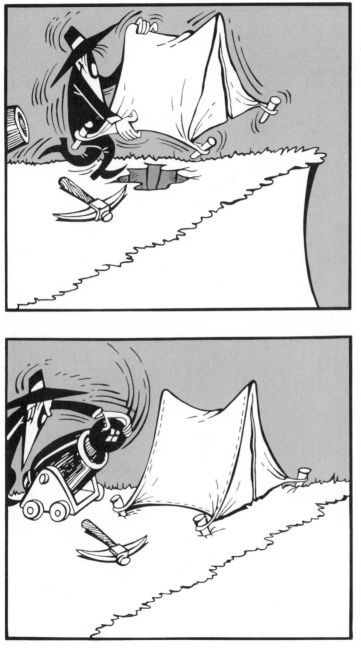

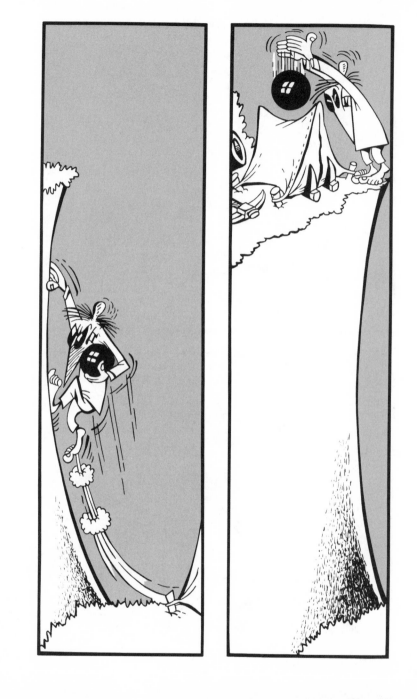

139

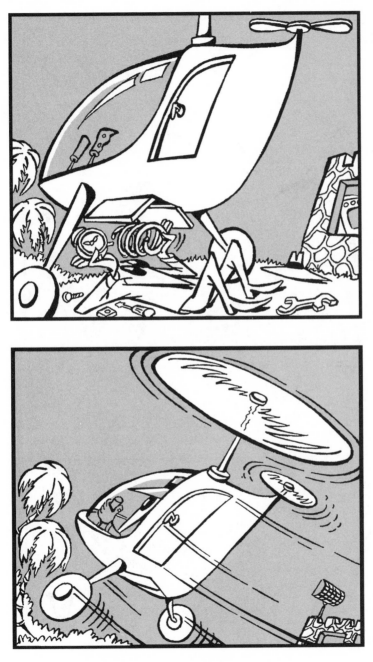

143

SPY VS SPY

144

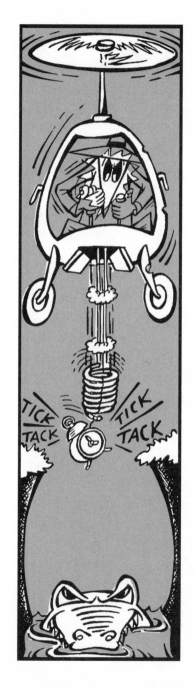

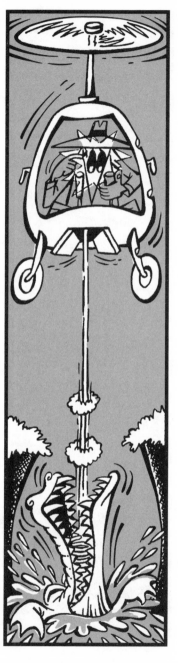

147

SPY VS SPY

154

Later

157

Still Later

SPY VS SPY

160

SPY VS SPY

164

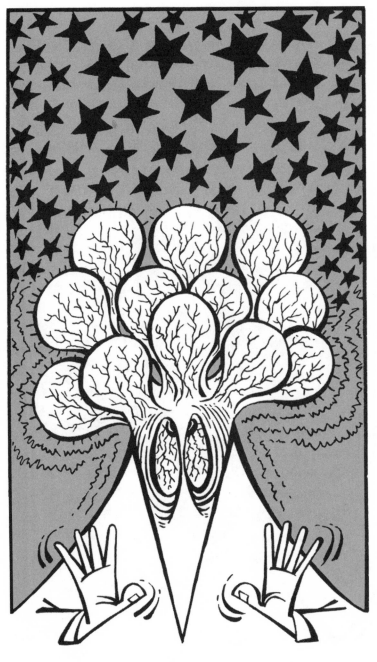

165

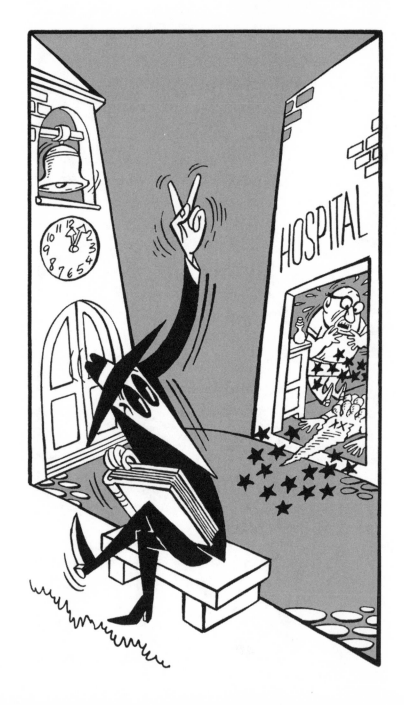

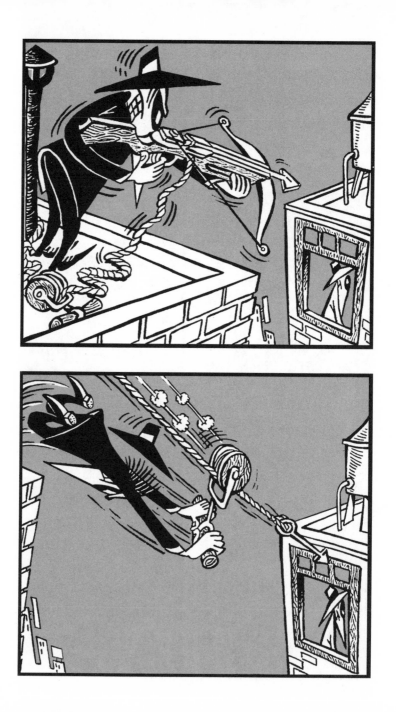

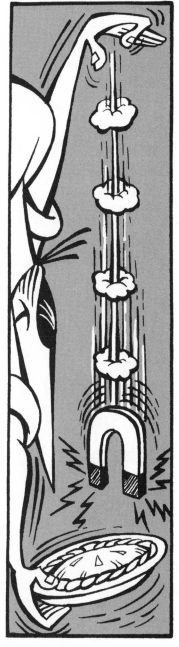

173

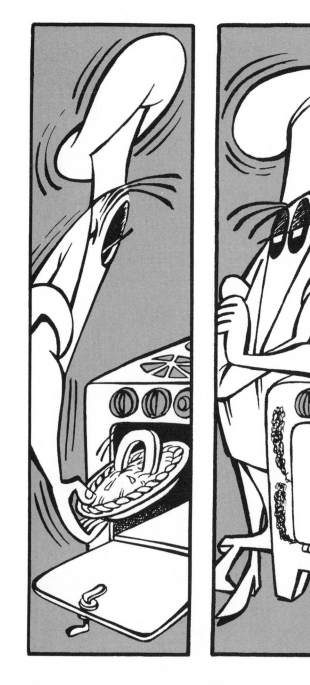

175

SPY VS SPY

178

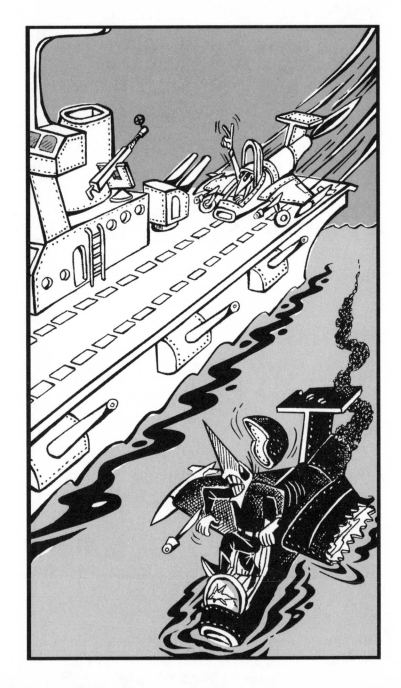

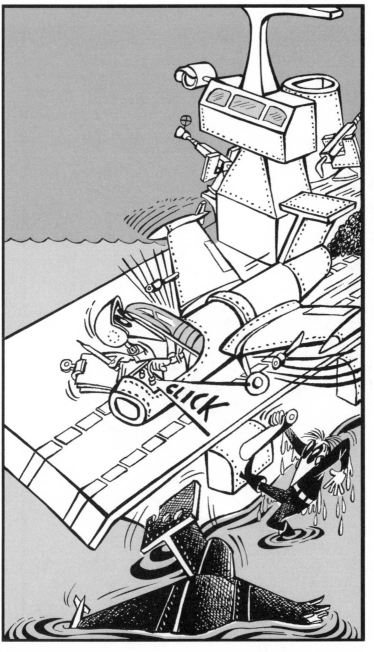

SPY VS SPY

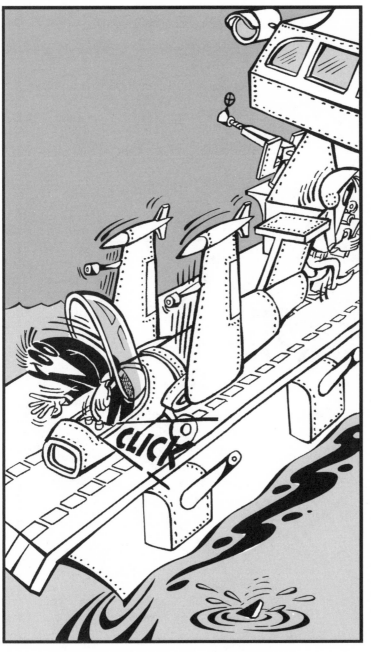

THE CARRIER-PIGEON PLOY

189

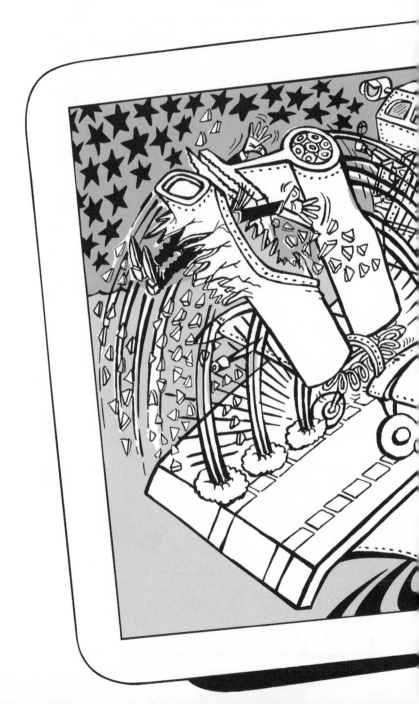

193

SPY vs SPY

the TWO ON THE ISLE FILE

195

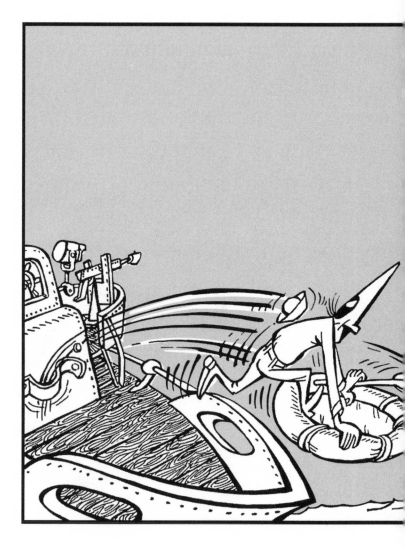

SPY VS SPY

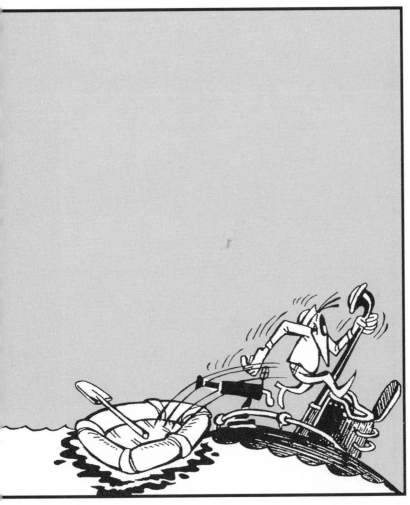

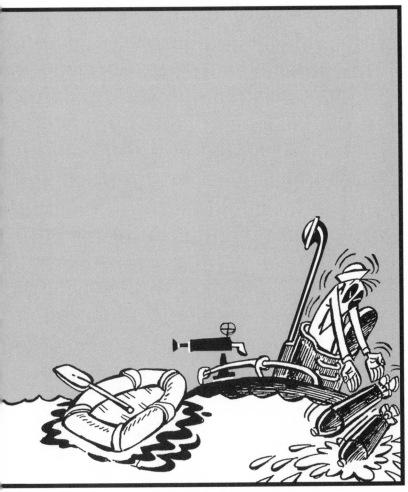

207

215

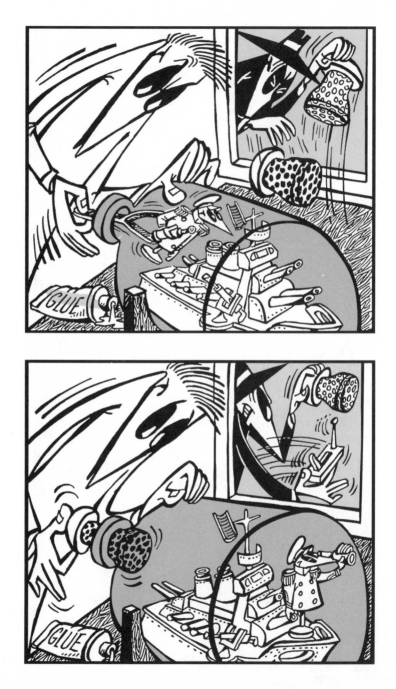

SPY VS SPY

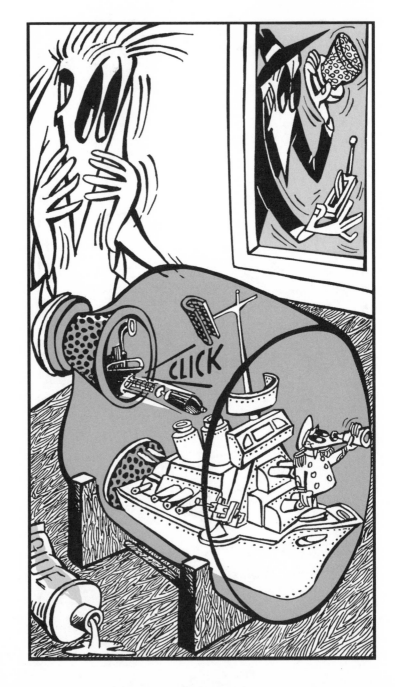

219

SPY VS SPY

220

221

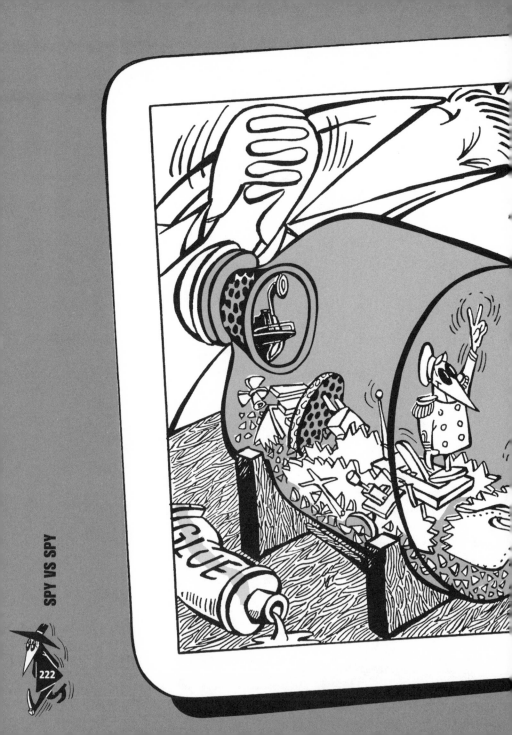

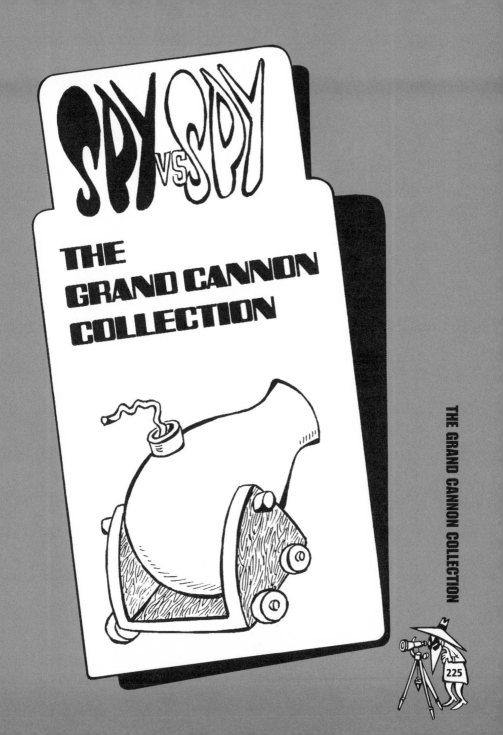

THE GRAND CANNON COLLECTION

225

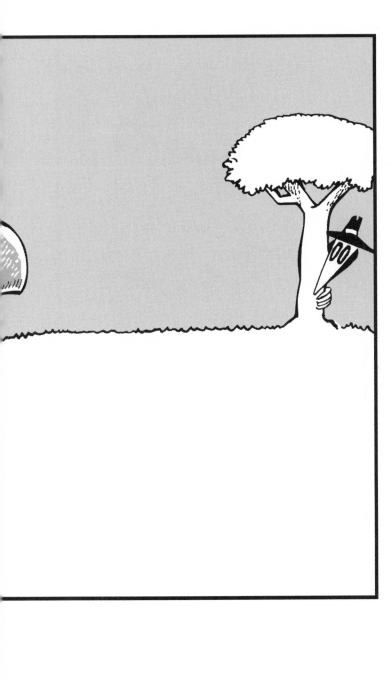

THE GRAND CANNON COLLECTION

227

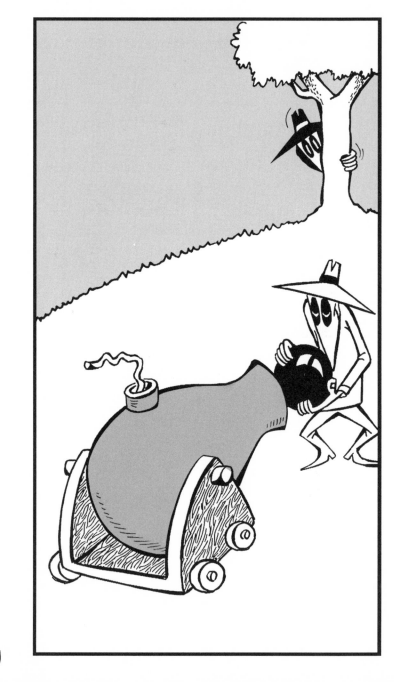

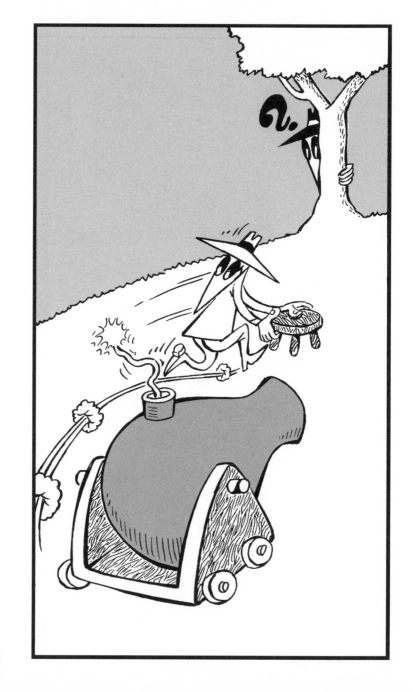

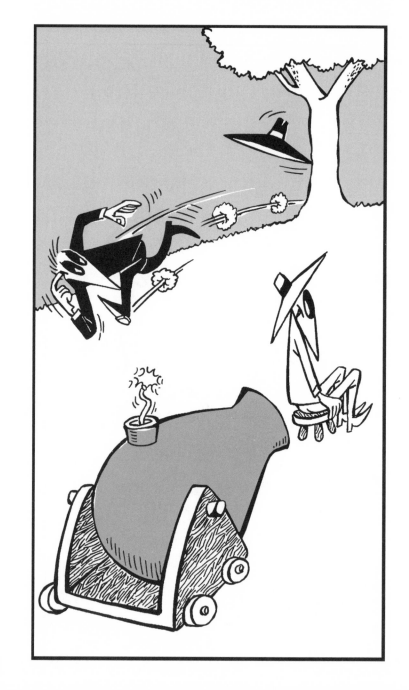

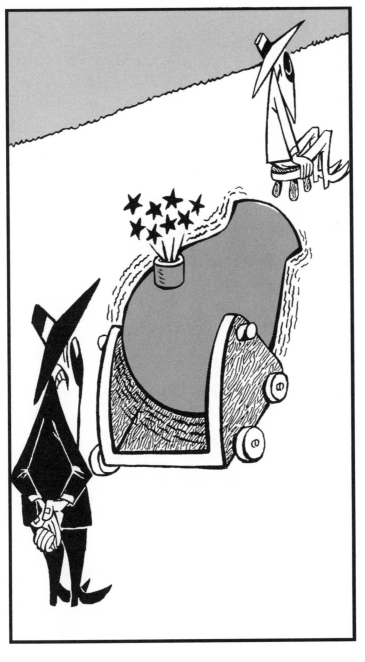

THE GRAND CANNON COLLECTION

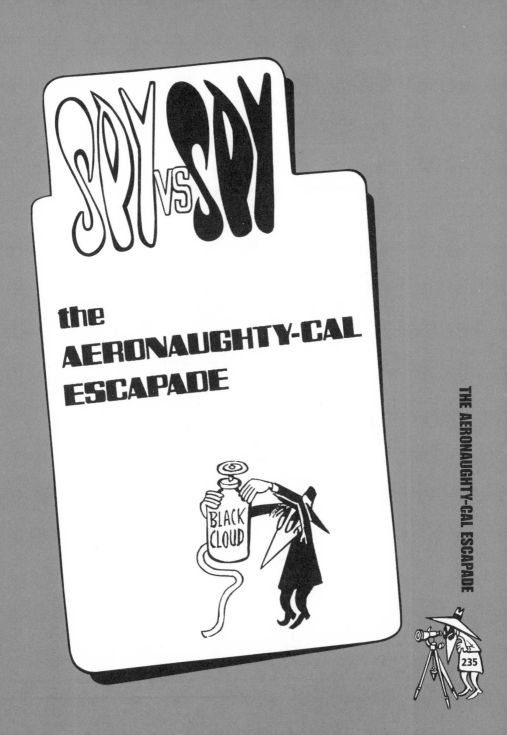

SPY vs SPY

the AERONAUGHTY-CAL ESCAPADE

236

237

THE AERONAUGHTY-CAL ESCAPADE

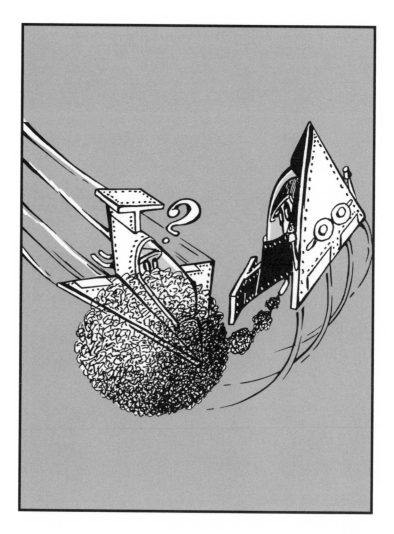

SPY VS SPY

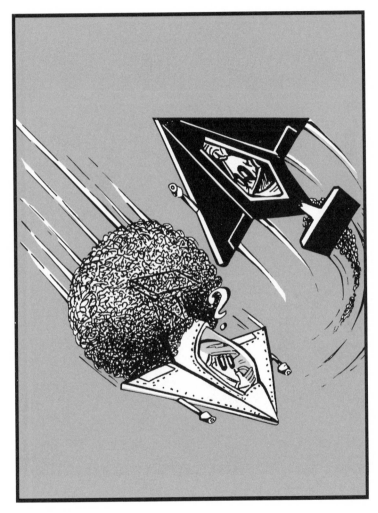

241

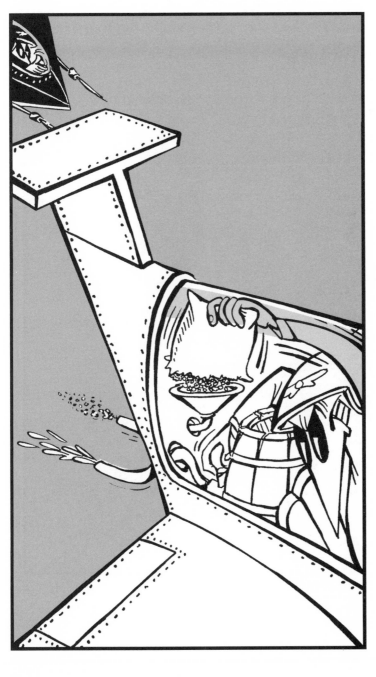

THE AERONAUGHTY-CAL ESCAPADE

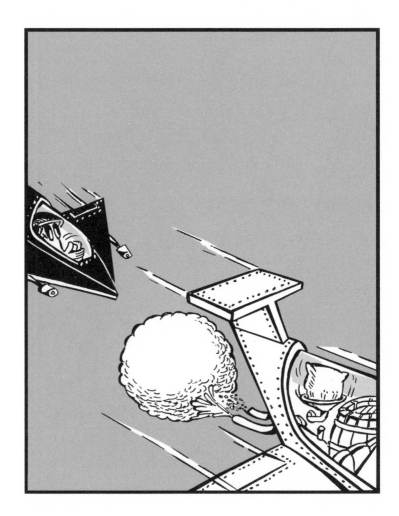

244

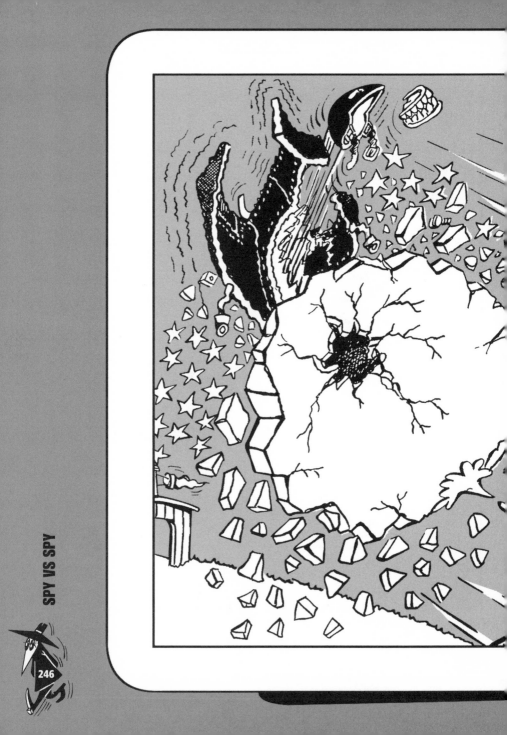

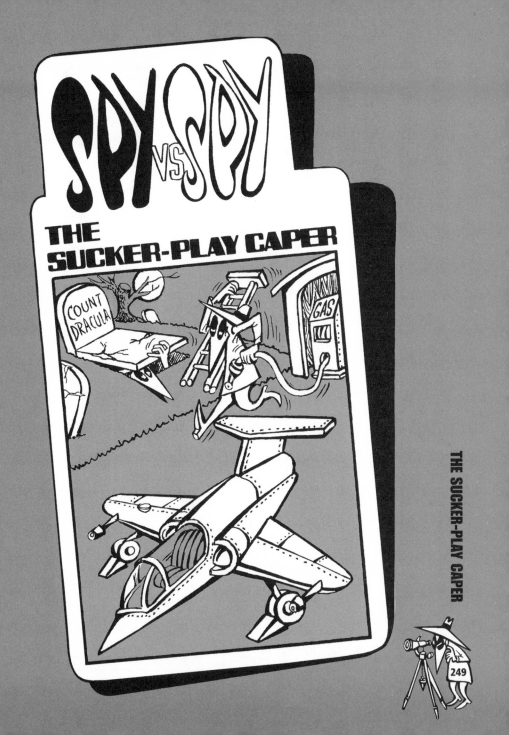

SPY vs SPY

THE SUCKER-PLAY CAPER

251

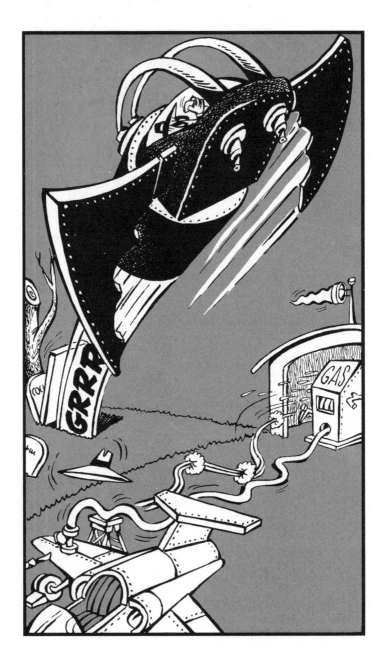

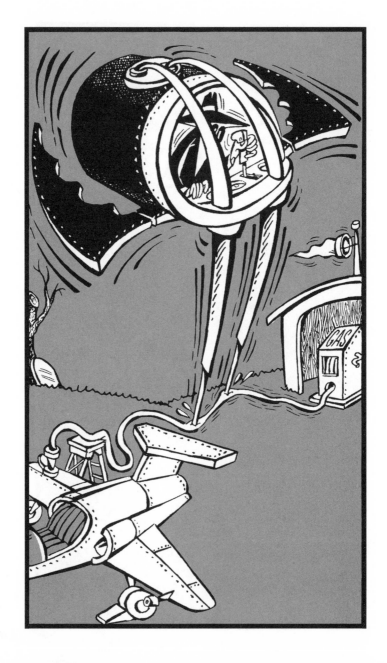

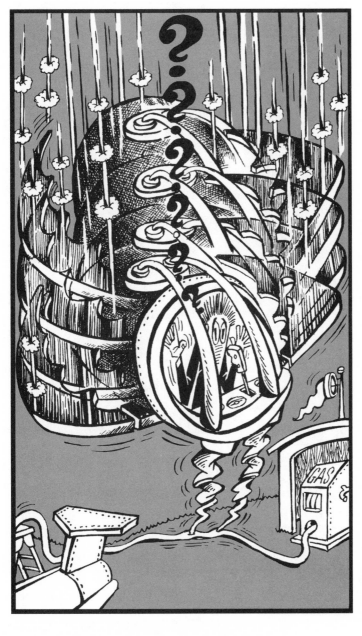

255

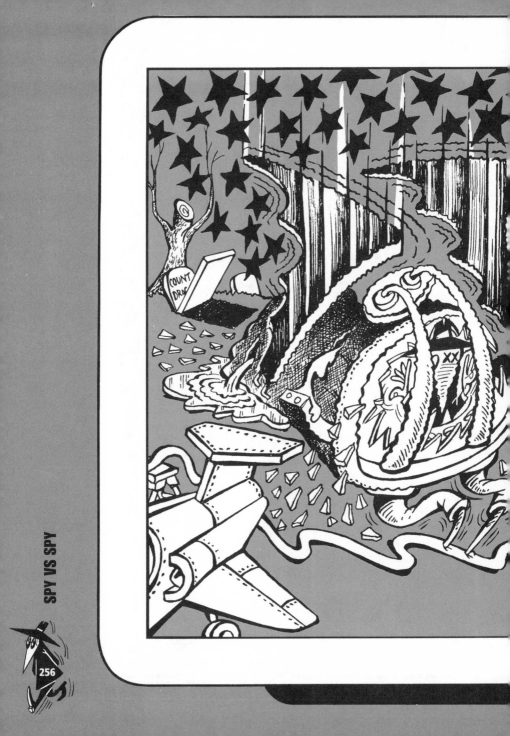

SPY vs SPY

the FLOAT-SOME and JET-SOME DOSSIER

261

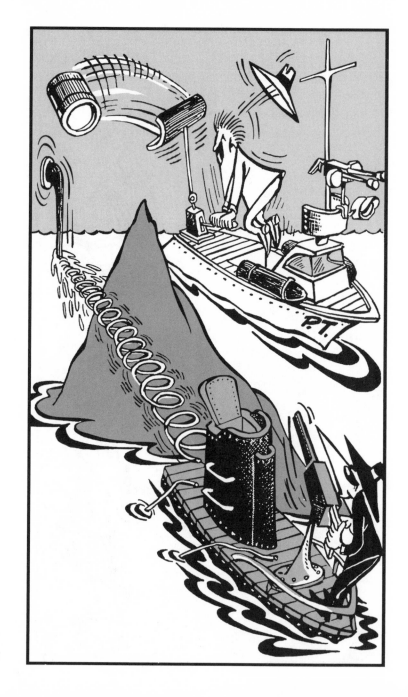

265

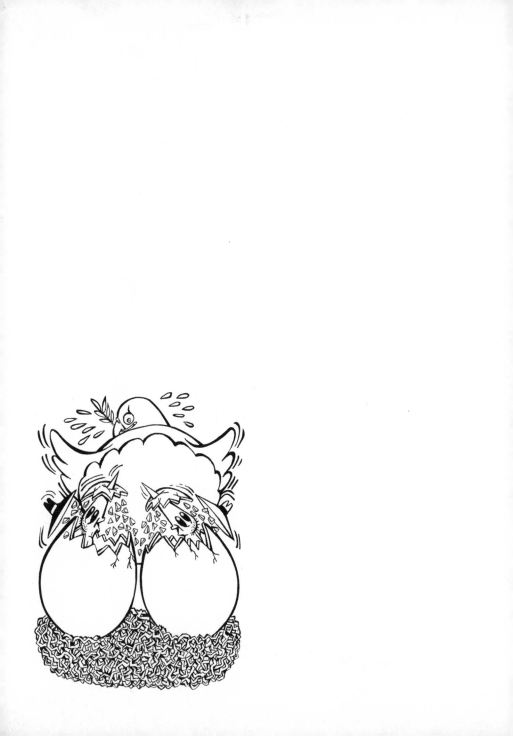

269

SPY VS SPY

270

271

273

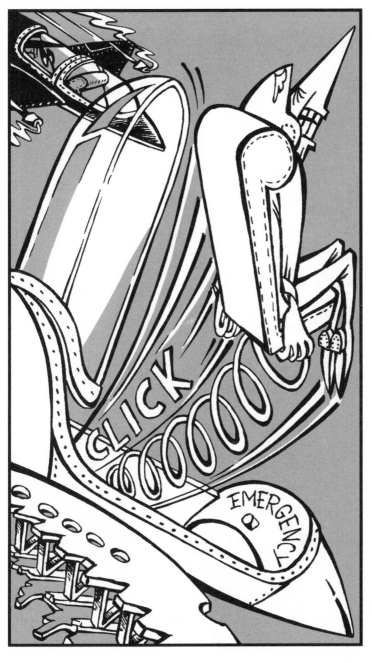

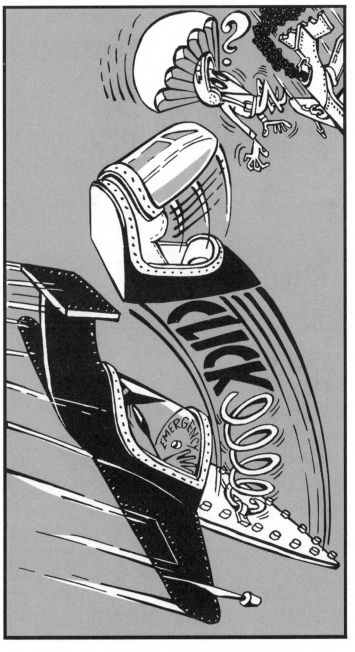

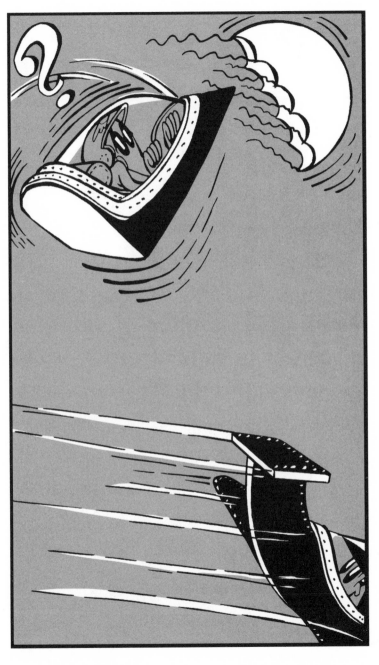

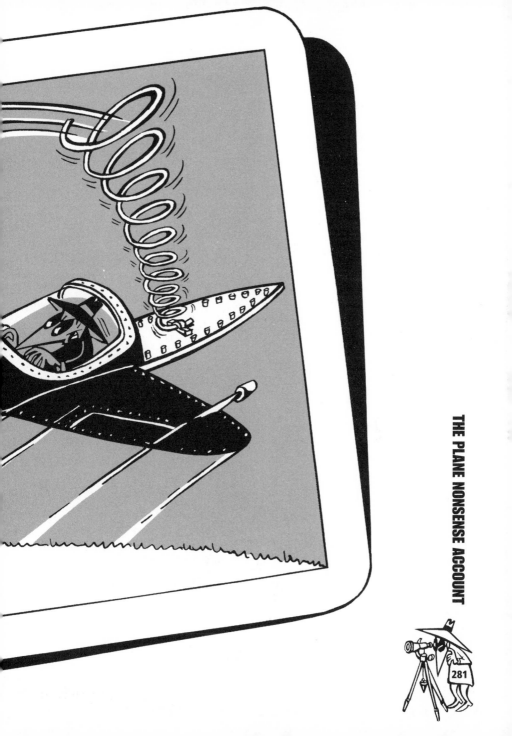